How to Start and Run a Successful Home Daycare Business

Tips from an Expert

Copyright 2018, Christina Kamp. All Rights Reserved

https://littlesproutslearning.co/

Dedication

This book is dedicated to my daughter, Kayla and my husband, Kent who have endured living in a daycare for most of their lives and supported me in my dreams and adventures.

Child Care-The Future Begins Here…

Table of Contents

Chapter 1	Page 7
Chapter 2	Page 8
Chapter 3	Page 11
Chapter 4	Page 12
Chapter 5	Page 14
Chapter 6	Page 19
Chapter 7	Page 25
Chapter 8	Page 29
Chapter 9	Page 35
Chapter 10	Page 44
Chapter 11	Page 59
Chapter 12	Page 65
Chapter 13	Page 66
Chapter 14	Page 67
Conclusion	Page 70
Resources	Page 73

How to Start and Run a Successful Home Daycare Business

Tips from an Expert

Do you love kids and think you could make a good living caring for them? You're in the right place. Over 20 years' experience taught me so much. I have learned what policies to have, expenses to consider, what schedules work best and what supplies and equipment you need. The information presented in this book will help you decide if a home daycare business is right for you.

Chapter 1-Home

Make sure your home is suitable for watching children. Is there enough room for several children to play? Do you have plenty of room to store all the daycare stuff? Is your home a safe environment for young children?

Take a look around your home, even sit on the floor or crawl on your hands and knees and check out the places you normally don't see. Make sure there aren't places where children can get hurt. If there are, what can you do to fix them?

Is your yard big enough for kid's toys and for them to run and play? Is it fenced in? Do you have pets out there? Is there a way to give them a separate area or will you have to poop scoop every day before the kids can come out?

Is your family on board with having extra kids in the house? Does your husband like the idea of having kids in the home when he gets off work? Will your kids be okay with sharing their house and their mom? What about their toys?

Do you have pets that are aggressive? Does your cat scratch everyone or your dog bite? Do your pets enjoying playing with kids? Are they patient with kids who are learning to be gentle? Do you have snakes or other reptiles in your home? If you do, is there a way to make them inaccessible to the kids you care for? Also, remember many parents won't want to do business there if you do.

Do you have room to store all the necessary supplies? You'll have to have some totes or closets, or a garage or something to fit all of the things necessary for the job. You don't want all of the "stuff" to suffocate you and your family.

If you think your environment will work for a home daycare, keep moving forward.

Chapter 2-Provider

Do you love kids? Are you patient with them while they are learning? Are you going to be okay with them tearing up your things and putting a lot of wear and tear on your home and furniture? In truth, they put a lot of wear and tear on you as well. Are you up for that?

What are your beliefs about discipline? Are you able to nurture kids as they learn, or are you unforgiving and harsh? Young children need lots of understanding and patience. They need a provider who will love them like their own children.

Do you get along well with other adults? In family childcare you will have to be able to stand up for yourself because a lot of parents try to take advantage. You'll also have to do it nicely or you won't have any business. You'll have to know what your rules are going to be ahead of time and prepare for what you'll do when someone wants to ignore them.

Are you able to express yourself in a calm and professional manner, even when someone owes you money or breaks your policies? What if they insult your family? Or your home? They will! There are so many wonderful parents out there, but you have to take the good with the bad. You'll have to know how to deal with people and still remain a professional businesses person. It takes some practice.

Are you reliable? Parents will need to go to work. Your grandma can't die every other week so you can have a break. You can't take off sick every time you break a fingernail. You have to be available as much as humanly possible. Things do come up, but you have to go the extra mile.

You need to be honest with people as well. People can tell when you're not being genuine and that's a big complaint I hear from parents about other providers. If you do something wrong, admit it. If a parent doesn't like how you do something, be truthful and let them know that's your procedure and you're not going to change it. You'll avoid a lot of problems this way.

Are you a safety person and a rule follower? Rules are in place for a reason. They keep things running smoothly. Trying to avoid the rules will only hurt you and the families you serve. If you are constantly getting caught doing something that's not best practices, word will get out about it.

Check out the checklist in the document pack to see if home daycare might work for you.

Daycare Checklist

- [ ] Enough room-
  35 square feet of open space per child indoors
  75 square feet of open space per child outdoors

- [ ] Storage-Toys, supplies, bedding, paperwork, files

- [ ] Toys-Ample indoor and outdoor toys for multiple kids

- [ ] Family and Pets-Will their temperament be good for a group of rowdy kids

- [ ] Temperament-Do you love kids, have patience with them, want to learn, are you okay with wear and tear on your things

- [ ] Professionalism-Are you able to be firm but patient with families even when their behavior is not great

- [ ] Reliability-Can people count on you, are you consistent, honest and organized enough to keep track of the mounds of paperwork involved

If you have a lot of love to give and want to be a great help to families, you may be a good fit for child care in your home. Not everyone can handle daycare. Some people are better working with kids in centers because the solitary life isn't good for them. That's okay.

But if you think you are a good fit for this kind of job, let's talk about some of the drawbacks of childcare. No rose colored glasses here.

Chapter 3-Drawbacks of family childcare

Home daycare is very isolating. You'll be working 10 hours a day with very little adult conversation.

It pays very little. You might bring in decent money, but the expenses for the job are huge.

There are no benefits like insurance or vacation pay. You can charge for your vacations but a lot of parents don't like that. It's up to you how you run your business though.

There are no breaks, no lunch hours, you can't run errands or go to the bathroom by yourself.

You can't call in sick without putting out several families. If you don't work, they can't go to work, so many times you will have to work sick.

Your kids may not want to share their rooms or their mom.

Your spouse may think they are okay with the daycare, but then complain relentlessly.

There is SO MUCH STUFF you need for the job.

Do you think you'll have tons of time to get your chores done? Think again, you'll be busier than you ever thought possible.

The paperwork can be suffocating.

It's difficult to schedule appointments for the doctor or anything else. Car repairs, dentist, going to the bank, and anything else that's not open late in the evenings. It's even hard to buy stamps.

There will be a ton of errands to run, but you can't leave to run them.

You miss many school events for your own child.

It takes a large initial investment in upgrades, toys, equipment and supplies.

Chapter 4-Laws and License

So, you think you can handle all the draw backs and you're ready to go into business for yourself. You can have a successful daycare. I have been running my home business for 23 years and have always been very successful. I'll share my secrets with you about how I did that and how I've always been full of kids with a waiting list.

What is the first step in getting started?

Check out what the law is in your area. In Oklahoma, you cannot even keep one child in your home without a license. The laws differ in other states. Some states have levels depending on how many kids you want to keep. Some laws charge for licenses, some don't. Find out what you need to do to be legal. Having an illegal daycare is not good for you or the families you serve. What happens if you get caught and shut down? Are there fines? Jail time?

Here is a website that will help you find regulations that apply to you where you live. https://childcareta.acf.hhs.gov/licensing

Find out what the procedures are to get your license. Where I live, you go to DHS and get a packet. You attend an orientation where they explain the rules. Then you read over the rules, make necessary changes in your house, prepare for inspection, sign up to be observed and wait for your appointment time.

DHS sends over the licensing specialist who goes through all the areas of your home and inspects everything. Then you will get a list of things you need to do to open. You can do those things and be issued a permit to operate for 6 months. During your permit time you will have more inspections to see if you will get a license.

Once you have your license you will have a surprise visit several times a year to make sure you are still doing what you are supposed to be doing. This continues until you quit. They are always unscheduled, so you never know when they are coming.

Liability Insurance

Your homeowner's insurance does not cover your daycare business. It covers damage such as fire, storm, etc. You can get enhancement insurance on your regular home owners policy or if you care for more than three children, or you can get general liability insurance for your business.

Enhancement usually covers business property, loss of income if something happens to your house and basic liability for accidents or injury. This type of insurance will not protect you in a lawsuit.

General liability insurance may cover immediate medical care at the time of an injury, physical injury, sickness, pain and suffering and death, damage to other people's property, the cost of legal defense, monetary amounts awarded to another party, child abuse and third parties (other people who live or work in your home).

Check with multiple companies to find a policy that meets your needs. Make sure you understand completely what is covered. Having insurance protects you from things that may come up.

Chapter 5-Rates and profit

What are the rates in your area? It's not legal to call providers and ask their rates. It's considered price gouging. You can find out rates by checking the DHS rates in your area and setting your rates according to that. What will DHS pay you to watch kids on subsidy? That will give you an idea of where to start. You can charge whatever you want. It can be more than subsidy, less or the same. It's up to you.

In Oklahoma, we can call our Resource and Referral and get a market rate survey result for the high and low rates for childcare in our area. If you have one, check that out.

You are allowed to inquire about child care rates for your own child. If you have a young child, you can be interested in what it would cost for their daycare needs. Once you find out the median price for child care in your area, decide if you want to specialize in something and charge a little more, or if you want to be average priced or go a little lower for lower income families.

There is a place in child care for all price ranges. You just have to decide what type of families you want to be serving. There is need at every price range.

Can you make a profit?

Let's make a hypothetical business plan

If you watch 6 kids at $150/week=$900/week

If you are open for 50 weeks a year and don't charge for your two weeks of vacation (you can charge for your vacations but not everyone does) $900 x 50=$45,000 brought in.

If you are on the food program and you are reimbursed for $500 a month in food $500 x $6,000

This brings your total income to $51,000 a year.

If you spend:

$7,000 a year on food

$1000 a year on advertising

$1000 a year on office supplies (this is very conservative with all the paperwork you'll have to do and copies you'll have to keep of everything)

$4,000 on supplies like paper products, extra household items and things you have to have to run the business day to day not including what you had to get to open

$3,000 more on household and yard expenses

$4,000 a year on activities for the kids

$1000 a year on training and other forms of education such as books and magazines to learn better ways to run your business

$3,500 more a year on upkeep of your house and repairs and maintenance that you wouldn't have had to do if the kids weren't there

$2,000 a year on toys and books (they get broken and wear out much faster than you think they will)

$850 a year replacing other equipment that wears out

$1,000 a year on gifts for daycare families and the kids

$1,000 a year on parties or special events for the kids or families or both

Your utilities (water and electric) go up $100 a month. $100 x 12 = $1200

That's a total of $29,250 in expenses not including insurance, big expenses like outdoor play equipment or replacing all of your sleeping mats or cots, or anything else major you'd need to do.

Subtract that from your income of $51,000 and you are making a profit of $24,150.

Next, deduct expenses for insurance, several thousand dollars for gas and car expenses to get to trainings and run all the errands you'll have to run to bring in all these supplies, and any other expenses that come up throughout the year. Let's say they add up to $6,000 more dollars for all of those miscellaneous things.

Now you made a profit of $18,150. Remember the national average is $16,000 a year.

You set your hours at 7:30-5:30, Monday through Friday. (Most providers work longer than this because everyone needs different hours. An average is Monday through Friday 6-6. For years I stayed open 7:30-6:30 and it was awful! I would never be able to do 12-hour days. Ten hours a day wears me out and I work a lot more hours when the kids aren't here.

You'll need to clean up after them every day, prepare meals and lesson plans, your training hours, meal planning, and the PAPERWORK! Now you're averaging 12-14 hours a day. So, for our example, we'll say 12 hours a day.

Take that 60 hours a week and multiply it by our same 50 weeks and you are working 3,000 hours a year. Monday through Friday 8-5 jobs are 2080 hours a year, do you see a big difference there? I know I feel every extra hour, especially now that I'm getting older.

Take your $18,150 a year and divide it by those 3,000 hours and you are working for $6.05 an hour. Far below minimum wage. Personally, I don't charge $150 a week and I don't charge for my vacation days and I take more than 2 weeks a year off, so my profit is not this big.

When people say it's a money-making venture or man, you sure make a lot of money, it takes me back because I just don't. I love what I do and it's a labor of love, not a get rich scheme. I was born to do it and I am happy and very fulfilled. My bank account however, is not so satisfied.

Don't forget if you have children who pay with subsidy from the government, every time they are absent, you don't get paid. That adds up quick! Sick days, vacation days, vacations for them. Every time they miss, you lose part of that profit.

The food program is the same. Every day someone doesn't show up, you lose money. You already bought the food, but no one is there to eat it and you don't get to claim it or get reimbursed for it. It does add up over the year.

If you make a mistake on your food program paperwork, you lose income. If your parents decide to leave owing you money, you lose income. Don't forget to account for the fact that you might not always have 6 kids enrolled, or 7 or 8 or 5 or whatever your capacity is. You can never count on any income until you have it in your hand.

This is just an idea of what it could be like. There are always many variables. Decide what you want to charge and how many kids you can keep and go from there. Then decide if you could be able to make enough profit to live.

Check the document pack for a spreadsheet to check your profit potential.

Daycare Income Calculator-Sample

# Kids		Weekly Rate			Weeks/Yr	Total/Yr
7	x	125	875	x	50	43750

Food Program		Months/Yr				Total/Yr
500	x	12				6000
					Total Income	49750

Expenses

Income		.80 (80% of inc.)				Total/Yr
49750	x	0.8				39800

					Income	49750
						-
					Expenses	39800
				Yearly	Tentative Profit	9950

Daycare Income Calculator

# Kids		Weekly Rate			Weeks/Yr	Total/Yr
	X			X		

Food Program		Months/Yr				Total/Yr
	X	12				
					Total Income	

Expenses						
Income		.80 (80% of inc.)				Total/Yr
	X	0.8				
					Income	
						-
					Expenses	
				Yearly	Tentative Profit	

Chapter 6-Equipment and supplies

There is a ton of stuff you have to have to be in business. These are a few things I have thought of, but it's certainly not an all-inclusive list. There may be more depending on regulations and what kinds of things you want to do with your kids.

First aid kit

Smoke detectors for every room kids will be using

Carbon monoxide detector

Fire extinguisher near kitchen

Emergency preparedness kit

Cleaning supplies

Really good vacuum

Mop or steamer

Hand Sanitizer

Soap dispenser

Paper towels

- Step stool
- Potty seat
- Child sized furniture
- Booster seats and high chairs
- Nap mats, cots or cribs
- Sheets, pillows and blankets
- Stuffed animals
- Storage items
- Outdoor play equipment
- Blocks
- Dramatic play toys
- Puzzles
- Arts and craft supplies
- Easels
- Smocks
- Glue
- Paint
- Paint brushes
- Crayons
- Popsicle sticks
- Feathers
- Scrap paper
- Construction paper
- Big paper
- Yarn
- Buttons
- Markers

Colored pencils

Chalk

Sidewalk chalk

Bubbles

Scissors

Cars and trucks

Dolls

Mirrors

Puppets

Hats

Dress up clothes

Kitchen stuff

Toy phones

Stuffed animals

Farm toys

Train set

Mr. Potato Heads

Games

Doctor kit

Bags and purses

Instruments

Posters for the wall

Water table

Measuring cups

Eye droppers

Funnels

Straws

- Magnifying glasses
- Magnets
- Seeds
- Lacing cards
- Dressing boards
- Playdough
- Riding toys
- Printer
- Computer
- Record keeping spreadsheets, notebooks or computer programs
- Something to play music
- Shelving
- Kid dishes including sippy cups and bottles
- Pack and play
- Bouncy seat
- Exersaucer
- Baby Swing

Of course, there are many more things you could have for kids to use at your home and you don't have to have every one of these, but you do need a wide variety of learning tools and supplies to run any business. Daycare is no different. It takes a lot to create an engaging environment for kids.

Ninja tip-You don't need to have a ton of things out at once. Less is more with kids. Just give them a few choices of materials to use and allow them to be creative. If you are having behavior problems or the kids never want to pick up, try boxing up some of the toys and storing them. I'm willing to bet you'll see a decline in that. There will be more interest in exploring the toys and less interest in just dumping them everywhere.

Changing station and bathroom supplies

Your back will LOVE you if you have a changing table for diaper changing. You don't have to, you can use a kinder mat on the floor if you like. They have cool changing tables that kids can climb up on themselves, but they are way out of my budget, so I have a step stool next to my changing table and I hold the kid's hand while they climb up on it. This way I can lift them from the top step instead of from the floor.

It helps them develop gross motor skills and it saves me from putting my back out. Lifting 3-7 kids multiple times a day from the floor to the top of the table can be hard on your body.

Changing tables or surfaces on the floor or wherever should be non-porous and sanitizable. You need to be able to spray them with sanitizer (the same one you use for the kitchen is fine) solution and leave it for one minute. Then wipe it dry. This is super important between kids. You don't want to spread illness from child to child.

You'll need diapers, wipes, gloves and diaper cream available at your changing station. For potty training you'll need changes of pants and underwear (socks and shirts are good to have too) and wipes. You'll also need plastic bags to send home clothing from accidents.

In the bathroom, you'll need a soap dispenser and paper towel dispenser. If you use individual towels, you'll need multiple hooks to hang them on and a way to tell who's whose are. They each need their own drying towel to prevent the spread of germs.

I love having wall hanging dispensers like public restrooms have. It keeps the soap from falling on the floor all the time and helps the kids use less soap and paper towels for less waste.

My husband found my paper towel dispenser at the thrift store and I bought a soap dispenser that makes ordinary soap into foam at the janitor supply store. I use organic soap because their soaps crack all the skin off my hands and give me rashes and the smell makes me sick. It just takes a small amount of soap to make a lot of foam for the kids.

I recommend using a foamer because kids like to squirt out a lot of soap and it's really hard to rinse it all away, clean it off surfaces and get it all off their hands if it's not foam. You'll also save a ton of money in wasted soap.

If you want to have the kids brush their teeth before nap, you can hang toothbrush holders in your bathroom too. I used to, but it was so hard for the kids to tell their brushes apart. There was too much cross contamination, so I stopped providing them.

One last thing you'll want to think about is bottles. Do you want to provide bottles or have parents bring them? Do you want to have parents bring premixed bottles daily, or do you want to have them provide a can of formula or bags of frozen breastmilk weekly?

I strongly suggest if you have a breast-fed baby, you have the mom provide bottles of milk instead of frozen bags. It's hard to not have those bags leak and spill. They get dinged up in the freezer and when thawing, the milk goes everywhere.

You can also decide whether you want to have one bottle per baby that you wash out multiple times a day or if you want a set of bottles and just throw them in the sink after each use. Whether parents bring them or you buy them, it's good to think about how you'll want to do it.

Let's talk about curriculum for a minute. There are a ton of fancy ones you can order, but I find that the simplest way to plan one is chose a topic and find ideas on my own. I don't usually like what is available. I don't like to do a lot of cookie cutter crafts, I like process art and free play. So, I come up with my own themes.

I've been doing this a long time. I've never used store bought curriculum, but when I started, it was hard to come up with ideas. The blog has several themes you can look at to get you started. We have themes for butterfly/caterpillar, summer, gardening/plants, valentines, dental health and tons of other activities and themes. Check it out for inspiration.

You can use those until you get the idea and are ready to make up your own. What I like more about getting ideas online than buying pre-packaged curriculum is that I can pick and choose what I want to use and not feel like I'm wasting money.

Another great thing about our themes is that they are CHEAP because we like cheap and free! I use what I have around the house, upcycle and any other thing I can do to save time and money.

Chapter 7-Safety measures

Plug covers on EVERY plug keeps kids safer. Cabinet locks for cabinets you want to keep kids out of can be installed. Safety gates to block off stairs, heaters, fireplaces and other dangerous things are an absolute must.

You need a smoke detector in every room kids will use (not in bathrooms or the kitchen). You need a fire extinguisher near the kitchen. You will also need a carbon monoxide detector in the house. We are total electric so we don't need one, but other than that, everyone needs one.

Do you have stairs to the front porch, deck or anywhere? They must have a hand rail. Make sure all your windows have screens to keep bugs out or don't open them. Make sure all of your doors and windows stay locked so no one can get in and so kids can't get out when you're in the bathroom or something.

Make sure your yard is fenced in. We are required to have a sturdy fence that is at least 4 feet tall and has no openings over 4 inches anywhere. This way kids can't slip out between the slats or by the gate. Make sure you don't let kids play near the street. Teach them to hold hands near cars.

Make sure you don't have standing water anywhere. Kids can even drown in a bucket. Standing water also breeds mosquitoes which is a whole other problem. If you have a pond or pool, you'll have to have it fenced off with a sturdy gate and locked at all times.

Speaking of mosquitoes, let's talk about medication permission. If you are going to administer any medication to kids, parents need to bring it in its original container and sign a form for you to administer it. You also need a form like this for sunscreen, band aids, diaper cream, bug spray or anything else you're going to put on the kids that may cause some type of reaction. This covers you.

You cannot use your pool with the daycare kids in Oklahoma. If your kids have a trampoline, you cannot use that with the daycare kids either. Check your area's rules on that, but remember if you do use them, they are a safety hazard, so watch the kids closely.

I have one form for everything and parents choose what they want on the kids and what they don't when they enroll. Then if I need to use anything like some peroxide, I have permission already. I just text and make sure and then go ahead and use it if it's okay with them. If they want to leave a bottle of Tylenol or other medication here, I label it with the child's name and then we have it if it's needed.

Check the document pack for an editable template of the medication form. You can make it your own and print it out.

Medication Permission Form

Please check the items you give permission to have used on your child (Tylenol, Ibuprophen and Benadryl must be provided by you and in the original, unopened container labeled with the child's name when dropped off to be kept at childcare)

☐ Tylenol

☐ Ibuprophen

☐ Benadryl

☐ Peroxide

☐ Band-Aids

☐ Neosporin

☐ Bug Spray

☐ Sunscreen

☐ Diaper Cream

☐ Essential Oils

I give permission to _____ to use the above checked items on my child.

_____
Signature   Date

Any cleaners, medications, body products or other dangerous substances need to be kept out of reach and out of sight of children. You can lock them up or keep them in the top of a closet. I have my medications in a linen closet in a basket on the top shelf. I keep my cleaners in a cabinet above the washing machine in a basket. The basket helps me reach them in a hurry when I need to.

For kids under three, be mindful of anything they can choke on. Don't leave toys, coins or other small parts within reach of kids.

Heavy furniture needs to be anchored to prevent it from being pulled over by kids and it crushing them. You can get inexpensive anchors that screw into the studs on the wall and then into the back of the furniture at the top so it can't be pulled over.

Keep kids out of the kitchen when you're cooking and protect them from hot surfaces. Cook on the back burners if possible.

Make sure there is always drinking water available for kids to drink. When you are playing outside on a hot day, make sure there is shade to play in and water is available to keep kids hydrated and from getting over heated.

Check the playground before kids play for stinging insects, spiders, snakes or anything else that may harm them. You never know what will come in the play area during the night or when you're not looking. Check under play equipment for wasp nests and hiding snakes or other animals.

NEVER leave babies sleeping in a room with the door shut. Never let them sleep with pillows, blankets, or fluffy things that could asphyxiate them. Never let them sleep in swings, bouncy seat and ESPECIALLY car seats. The angle those products hold babies at are super dangerous for them. There are more safe sleep tips on the blog.

Always make sure to eat with the kids or supervise them when eating. Kids can choke so fast and you need to be there to help make sure their throat becomes cleared.

Store matches lighters, weapons and other dangerous thing under lock and key and out of sight. Make sure your water heater is set to 120 degrees or less to avoid burns from hot water.

Be mindful of cords that hang down off of appliances that kids can pull on or tablecloths that can be pulled off the table. Think about a hot pot of soup on a table cloth or something in the fryer on the kitchen counter. It's so easy for a preventable injury to occur.

Be mindful of your toys and art supplies. Make sure what they're made of is safe for kids. Think about food allergies and playdough. I had a child with multiple allergies eat some playdough. I didn't know if her allergies were in the playdough. I had to think fast to find the ingredient listing, but luckily, she was fine.

There are so many things you don't think about. Make sure art supplies are ASTM safe. Make sure toys aren't painted with lead paint (many from China are) or have small pieces that can break off and hurt kids or choke them.

Be prepared for emergencies. There are so many things that come up. Practice drills for tornadoes, fires, floods, and other times when caring for multiple children would prove difficult. Thinking through your plans can save a lot of time if the need comes up.

Think about things like impact materials under outside play equipment, securing rugs to the floor, covering sharp corners of furniture or other things that could injure children. It's better to be safe than sorry. Preventable injuries cause most deaths of children.

Chapter 8-The difference between daycare and awesome daycare

There is daycare and there is kick butt awesome daycare. My personal feeling is that if I'm going to be with kids 10 hours a day, why not rock those 10 hours. Now I don't mean I'm awesome for 10 hours a day, no, I'm not. I mean I want to do something to make each day meaningful.

I don't want to sit on the couch and watch tv while the kids play. I would hate myself and be so depressed if I only did that. I want to connect with the kids every day and make sure they know they are loved. I want them to feel like someone when they are here.

I think every child deserves a GREAT place to be.

I don't spend a ton of money on fancy equipment or toys, I use what I have until it falls apart. I cut down on waste as much as possible. I don't buy fancy paper plates for special events, I hate throwing dishes in the landfill. I use empty cereal boxes and things from the recycle bin for crafts and toys.

I don't buy fancy curriculum because none of it reflects my beliefs. I don't use a certain teaching style, I blaze my own trail. I lean towards a few styles of thinking, but nothing out there speaks to what I really believe all the way to the bottom of my soul.

I will recommend Dr. Becky Bailey Conscious Discipline-anything she writes or teaches. I will also recommend studying the Reggio Emilia approach to teaching-it's the closest to what I feel in my heart. We have a responsibility in early childhood to give kids the best start we can and birth to 3 is so important.

Developmentally appropriate practice is not practiced in public school, so it's up to us to set the standard and give kids as much as we can to start before they have to go to school.

What is the number one thing kids need for success in life?

PLAY!!!

During play children learn to solve problems, interact with other people, take turns, share, build, balance, create, imagine and so much more! Play is children's work! Kids need plenty of time to play unhindered, to imagine out scenarios, to work out problems between them. Play is the answer to later success in life.

Children learn 80% of what they will learn in their ENTIRE lifetime before they reach school. We have a lot of teaching to do. What is the NUMBER ONE indicator of future success for a child? SOCIAL SKILLS! Do they learn social skills from flash cards? NO. Do they learn them from work sheets? NO. Do they learn them from cookie cutter crafts that have to look perfectly alike? NO.

They learn these skills from pure simple play.

Creativity is formed by the time a child is age 8. In Oklahoma, art is not taught until the 5th grade…Let that sink in a minute. So, if creativity is not nurtured in school, where is it nurtured?

If we don't raise creative children, who will solve the world's problems? Who will come up with cures or create designs for new buildings or make more efficient cars or appliances? Who is going to come up with creative solutions for the problems of the future?

The answer is no one. Creativity is vital to our survival, we MUST nurture this in children. We don't do this by making a flag craft and coming around to each child's paper and straightening their stripes (essentially telling them they aren't good enough to make a flag) so they will all look the same. We do this by giving them paint and letting them smear it all over the paper however they want.

We nurture creativity by taking kids outside and letting them use a pile of sticks to build the Taj mahal. We do this by letting them use a bandana for a map. They need time to create, think and play. That's how our future will be better. That's how we raise world changers, strong thinkers, and adults who work well with others.

Most kids run through the Mc Donald's drive through on the way home and eat a happy meal in the car. Does that mean our efforts to make them really healthy food are wasted? HECK NO! It means they NEED us to make healthy food even more because it's the only healthy food they may get.

Kids eat 2/3 of what they get in their day when they are with us. They need all the nutrition they can get. If your kids won't eat healthy food, check out how I get mine to on the blog. Or get my book, Zero to Hero Nutrition. How to Actually Get Kids to Eat Healthy Food. Check it out on Amazon.

It has the tools I used to transition my family, myself and my daycare kids from junk food junkies to healthy eaters. It even worked for my husband. I promise, the techniques will help!

So, what, besides these things, separates a good daycare program from a great one? How have I always stayed full with a waiting list for over 23 years? Is it because I'm better than someone else? NO WAY!

Staying full is all about nurturing relationships. You are providing care for your parents just as much as you are for kids. You need to minister to the whole family. It's hard to drop your kids off with someone else. It's hard to work when you're worried about their wellbeing.

Moms and Dads need to know their kids are well and happy. They need to know everything is okay. Some people need a lot more of this than others. If you sense a parent is nervous, spend a little time helping them. I always text my parents pictures and reports at least a couple of times on their first day.

I take a quick pic with my phone and write what the kids are doing. It reassures them. If they are worried and ask how they are doing, I do it again. It just takes a few minutes and it's so reassuring to a worried parent.

Throughout their first week, I try to update parents once a day, unless they ask and then I do more. I don't want to drive them crazy at work, but I also don't want them to be distracted wondering. I always tell all parents they are welcome to ask any time. I don't want them to think it bothers me. I worry about my child and I like updates too.

Throughout their time here, I will send these updates occasionally. Once they get used to bringing them and used to me, I do it less than once a month. It still helps parents feel connected and know I care.

Another way you can support families is by being an encourager. Build them up. Every parent feels like a failure at some point. Some of us do the entire time. A few words like, your child has a good heart or they are smart or the treats you made were so cute and we appreciate it, goes a long way to help a parent feel like they are doing okay.

Don't make up stuff or lie, but even, I like that shirt he has on, is something supportive to say. Find something positive and tell them, or text them at least once a month about it. Every day is better, but ain't nobody got time for that.

If you need to approach a parent about a problem, sandwich it with positive things. Little Johnny is so smart and I want him to succeed. We are having a big problem with him hitting the other kids. I'd like some help from you in letting little Johnny know how to treat people. Can you talk to him and watch that closely please? I will report back with you if we are making progress with this problem or not. I really enjoy him and love his funny jokes. Thanks for your time.

It's not that hard to put a positive spin on things so parents don't feel threatened or overwhelmed. Life can already be overwhelming as it is. Show kindness, just the way you would want someone to show kindness to you.

Get parents involved. They will feel more invested in the program if you include them. Ask them for snacks for special occasions. You can have family events at your house where parents can meet each other and watch their kids interact. Send home construction paper and have parents trace and cut out everyone's feet and bring them back.

You can use them for sorting and counting, matching or color identification if you do a different color for each family. This is great for the kids because they feel connected to those feet as they remember doing this at home with their family. I do it and hang them on the wall like they are footprints walking all around the room. The families love it.

Anything you can do to involve parents, do it. Your program will grow because of it. People who feel invested talk about it to their friends and word of mouth is the number one way to get business in child care. Everyone wants a good reference, but especially for daycare.

Give the best of yourself. Don't do daycare as an afterthought. Put some planning into how to make your day go well. If you don't keep kids busy, they will keep you busy and it's usually not in a good way. Be the best you can be. Just like me, sometimes your best will suck, but some days you will knock it out of the park.

There is nothing like knowing you gave your best. Kids are the most important thing you can spend your time investing in. There is NOTHING more important than our future and kids are that future. What you give them sets the tone for their life more than anyone else in the world besides their parents.

Your influence makes a huge difference. Birth to 3 is the most influential time in a child's life and you have the chance to make that awesome and give them the foundation for great things. Take it seriously. Society doesn't view this job as important. It's just babysitting right? NO! It's the most important job in the world. Now get out there and be awesome!

Your reputation will get around quicker than you think and it can be for good things or bad. For the most part, that is up to you. What image are you putting out there? Do you get mad and yell at your parents, or do you treat each situation professionally?

I have been mad at parents many times, but I take a deep breath and handle it in the best way I can. I try to empathize, and not just be selfish. I try to come up with a solution too. Sometimes that can't be done, it's okay to move on. The main thing is to handle it like a grown up.

Use what you can to promote what you're doing. Do you friend your daycare parents on Facebook? I do. And I promote myself on there. If you don't, you can do it by text or email. It's hard to take the time to tell each family what you have going on with the kids, so use technology to help you. Newsletters are another way to keep parents informed. I find that most people use technology more easily and I get better results that way but use whatever works for you.

I post pictures and videos of what the kids are doing and show the community including my parents what we are learning. I also post about time I spend preparing for daycare. If I spend two full weekends working on my [taxes](#) or 3 weeks working on [lesson plans](#), I post it so people know the effort I put into the business. If I take training, I post it so people know I'm bettering myself for their kids. My parents love it and I get more contact for business than I could handle in 5 lifetimes.

Remember if you post kids on social media, you have to have signed releases from all your parents. There is an editable and printable copy of this form in the [document pack](#).

Multimedia Permission Form

I give my consent for _____ to use photographs or videos of my child on social media, blogs or websites and in books, magazines, newspapers and other publications.

I give _____ permission to publish, exhibit, and distribute these materials. I understand that _____ owns the copyright to the multimedia material in which my child may appear.

The images will convey positive images of children and not use these images in a harmful manner.

_____
Name of Child (print)

_____
Parent/Guardian Name (Print)

_____
Signature of Parent/Guardian   Date

What can you do to stand out from the crowd? Offer something different in your program. What are you interested in? Are you vegetarian? Be a vegetarian daycare. Are you Christian? Be a Bible based daycare. Do you love math? Offer a stem program in your child care. Do what you love and promote it to your potential clients.

Fill a need. Find out what everyone is looking for. Is there a shortage in your area for infant care? Specialize in that. Is there a need for structured preschool programs? Make one. Do people need help with after school care? Maybe that's your niche. What about keeping only teacher's kids and taking off one or two months in the summer? You could set your hours 7-4 and be off a week at Christmas too.

Do you know a ton of stay at home moms that need a day off in the week? Make a mom's day out program Monday through Thursday and offer care to multiple families one day a week. I have done so many different things over the years. Do what works for you and what there is a need for.

If you decide to do one of those things or something completely different, promote the heck out of that. Whatever makes you stand out as quality should be celebrated. Once people see you doing it, they will do it too when they talk about you and recommend you to their friends.

You have to respect what you're doing to celebrate it. If you think this is a loser job, it's not for you, do something else. If you decide to do daycare, KNOW that you are changing the world and be proud of it. No one will respect you if you don't respect yourself. If you don't respect what you're doing, you won't put effort into it and you won't love your job. Loving what you do and knowing it matters is the best feeling in the world.

Now, people are going to say negative things to you. Someone will say, why don't you get a real job or it must be fun to play all day. Those things hurt, but you just have to realize that's on them. It's their ignorance and no reflection on the truth.

Invest in yourself. You'll provide much better care if you spend time and energy getting educated. Make sure you try to better yourself. I was talking to a provider friend the other day and we were both remarking about how much better providers we are than we were back in the day.

We learn so much by spending time with kids and learning new information. We do better now because we know better. Invest in your future and the future of your kids by learning as much as you can.

Chapter 9-Daycare Menu

Once you get ready to enroll kids, you'll need to decide if you want to get on the food program. I say do it. It's lots of paperwork, but it's also free money. It's worth it. Don't cheat yourself out of extra income just because of some paperwork.

The food program is basically a good program that will help you feed your kids healthy food (for the most part) and give you training and extra money. Check online for food programs in your area and get signed up.

The food program has guidelines that you must follow for your meals. You'll need a cycle menu. This is a good idea whether you are on a food program or not. It will help you be organized and have the food you need on hand for the meals you feed the kids. DHS has feeding requirements for lunch anyway and in Oklahoma they are the same as the food program.

You'll have to have a meat or meat alternate, a bread, two vegetables or a fruit and a vegetable plus milk for lunch every day. For breakfast you can do a bread and a fruit or vegetable plus milk or you can do protein instead of bread and a fruit or vegetable plus milk up to 3 days a week.

Snack is a choice of two: milk, meat or meat alternate, bread, fruit or vegetable. You can choose any two you'd like. For infants under age one, there are different guidelines for feeding. The portion sized depend on the ages, so check with DHS or your food program to see what they are.

There is a ton of menu planning information on the blog as well as breakfast, lunch and snack ideas you can use. Check the document pack for an editable menu you can customize for yourself.

Weekly Menu Planner

Menu Number	Breakfast	Lunch	Supplement
1	WG Cereal Grapes Milk	Tuna Salad Tomatoes Pickles Crackers Milk	Crackers Peanut Butter
2	WG Toast Oranges Milk	Sausage Apples Carrots WG Biscuits Milk	WG Muffins Grapes
3	WG Pancakes Banana Milk	Boiled Eggs Salad Broccoli Crackers Milk	WG Cereal Raisins
4	WG Cereal Cantaloupe Milk	Grilled Cheese Squash Bananas WG Bread Milk Cottage Cheese	Pretzels Grapefruit
5	WG Muffins Raisins Milk	Taco Soup Bean Tomatoes Corn Tortilla Chips Milk	WG Bread Applesauce

Weekly Menu Planner

Menu Number	Breakfast	Lunch	Supplement
6	WG Toast Oranges Milk	Pigs in a Blanket Carrots Apples WG Biscuits Milk	Cheese Stick Cantaloupe
7	WG Cereal Bananas Milk	Mac and Cheese Beans Apples WG Noodles Milk	Pretzels Oranges
8	WG Muffins Raisins Milk	PB&J Sandwich Asparagus Bananas WG Bread Milk Cottage Cheese	Crackers Strawberries
9	WG Cereal Grapefruit Milk	Bean Burrito Lettuce Tomatoes WG Tortillas Milk	WG Toast Peanut Butter
10	WG Pancakes Blueberries Milk	Ground Beef Peas Oranges WG Noodles Milk	WG Cereal Peaches

Weekly Menu Planner

Menu Number	Breakfast	Lunch	Supplement
11	WG Cereal Bananas Milk	Scrambled Eggs Spinach Strawberries WG Bread Milk	WG Bread Oranges
12	WG Muffins Mixed Fruit Milk	Ham & Cheese Celery Corn Crackers Milk	Pretzels Applesauce
13	WG Pancakes Bananas Milk	Chicken Potatoes Salad Brown Rice Milk	Crackers Peaches
14	WG Cereal Raisins Milk	Cheese Pizza Tomato Sauce Salad WG Tortilla Milk	WG Muffins Carrots
15	Oatmeal Cherries Milk	Beans Cauliflower Oranges Cornbread Milk	WG Cereal Apples

Weekly Menu Planner

Menu Number	Breakfast	Lunch	Supplement
16	WG Cereal Mixed Fruit Milk	Quesadilla Green Beans Salad WG Tortillas Milk	Cheese Sticks Raisins
17	WG Toast Pears Milk	Chicken Corn Peas WG Noodles Milk	Pretzels Raisins
18	WG Pancakes Oranges Milk	Meatballs Bananas Potatoes WG Pasta Milk	WG Muffins Apples
19	WG Cereal Strawberries Milk	Beef Soup Apples Mixed Vegetable Crackers Milk	Boiled Egg Grapes
20	Oatmeal Raisins Milk	Empanadas Pineapple Carrots WG Crust Milk	Crackers Strawberries

Weekly Menu Planner

Menu Number	Breakfast	Lunch	Supplement
21	Scrambled Eggs Raisins Milk	Ham & Cheese Grapefruit Carrots WG Bread Milk	Crackers Cantaloupe
22	WG Muffins Cantaloupe Milk	Tuna Casserole Apple Peas WG Pasta Milk	Cheese Stick Watermelon
23	Cream of Wheat Apples Milk	Pizza Cucumbers Carrots WG Crust Milk	WG Muffins Blueberries
24	WG Pancakes Bananas Milk	Chs Pasta Salad Apple Green Beans WG Pasta Milk	Crackers Peanut Butter
25	WG Cereal Oranges Milk	Goulash Pineapple Corn WG Noodles Milk	WG Toast Apples

Weekly Menu Planner

Menu Number	Breakfast	Lunch	Supplement
26	WG Toast Grapes Milk	Cottage Cheese Bananas Carrots WG Pasta Milk	WG Muffins Raisins
27	Boiled Eggs Pears Milk	Hot Pockets Bananas Asparagus WG Crust Milk	Crackers Apples
28	WG Pancakes Bananas Milk	Cheese Raisins Peas Crackers Milk	WG Toast Oranges
29	Scrambled Eggs Cherries Milk	Chicken Stir Fry Cabbage Apples Brown Rice Milk	WG Toast Banana
30	Oatmeal Strawberries Milk	Roast Potatoes Broccoli WG Roll Milk	Cheese Stick Apples

Weekly Menu Planner

Menu Number	Breakfast	Lunch	Supplement
31	WG Muffins Peaches Milk	Sausage Balls Apples Mixed Vegetables WG Biscuit Milk	Crackers Strawberries
32	WG Cereal Bananas Milk	Hamburgers Watermelon Corn WG Bun Milk	WG Bread Raisins
33	WG Toast Apples Milk	Chicken Strips Potatoes Broccoli Crackers Milk	WG Muffins Peaches
34	WG Muffins Blueberries Milk	Cottage Cheese Peaches Greens Crackers Milk	Crackers Banana
35	WG Pancakes Watermelon Milk	Turkey Potatoes Carrots WG Roll Milk	Cheese Stick Raisins

Some things to remember when planning meals for kids:

Make sure there are different colors on the plate. An all yellow meal like cheeseburger mac, oranges and carrots is less appetizing than a colorful meal. Different colors of produce also offer different nutrients so make sure your kids are getting a variety of colors every day.

Make sure you are serving something that is warm and something that is cold in most of your meals. A variety of temperatures and textures helps kids want to try more things so keep it in mind.

Remember a few things about feeding kids. It takes 11 times of introducing a new food before it's not new anymore. You may find that kids will eat something after you offer it numerous times. It's okay for them to not eat everything on their plate. Forcing kids to clean their plate or encouraging them to make a happy plate can lead to eating disorders or obesity.

Meal times should be peaceful. It's best if adults sit with kids and eat with them. You can model good table manners and eating habits this way. If you just can't eat with the kids, make sure you are still supervising them.

At Little Sprouts, we have the rule that you can't say something is yucky. It hurts my feelings if people say my food is yucky and I want my kids to be polite when they go to their friends houses. I also want them to be kind to their parents and other people who feed them. We say, if you don't like it, just don't eat it. Nothing needs to be said.

Another rule we have is if you want seconds, you have to wait for me to get done eating and ask you if you want more. The problem with giving everyone whatever they want whenever they want it is twofold. Number one, they should learn to be patient and wait for someone to be ready to offer them more. Everything we do shouldn't be on the child's time. Everyone can't be first or the center of attention when it's you and 7 kids. I want my kids to learn manners and patience and to treat someone who is feeding them kindly.

The second reason is there are 7 of them and one of me. By the time I finish filling 7 plates for 7 kids, the first one is done and ready for seconds. If I was at their beck and call with seconds, I would never get to eat. It's super important to me to eat with the kids. Like I said before I can model good habits for them, but also, I feel like meal time is THE BEST time of the day to have great conversations.

When we are eating the kids tell me about their evening the night before or things about how they feel or what they are thinking. This is super important to me. I WANT my kids to talk to me and tell me everything. I love that they feel that way about me and want to share. I always want to have those times when we can just have great conversations together.

Chapter 10-Contract and policies

A contract is a must have for your business. I did daycare for a few years without it but when I made one and started using it with families, my new clients treated me with far more respect and like a business owner instead of a babysitter.

It's important to view what you're doing as a business and treat it like one. Contracts protect you and set up expectations for both parties that are more reasonable. Your parents know what matters to you when you set it up in your contract.

A contract covers time and money, policies are for everything else. With contracts and policies, the shorter the better. If you want people to read and pay attention to what you put in there, don't go on and on about everything. Choose what really matters to you and stick to just that. Your contract should be one page or less if at all possible.

The things it should cover include:

Your business hours

Your holiday and vacation policies

Your rates and when they are due

Your other fees

Anything else that's a deal breaker for you.

Simple and to the point.

There should be a place for parent's signature and yours as well as the date. You are both agreeing to a binding contract.

There is an editable contract in the document pack.

Contract for Child Care Services

The following is an agreement between _____ and the parents of:_____

Hours of business are _____

I am closed for the following **paid** holidays:

Payment will be made during child's absences.

I will take at least fifteen days vacation per year. Two weeks notice will be given before vacation. <u>Payment will not be required for **my** vacation days.</u>

Weekly rate: $ _____   Payment will be made: _____

<u>**Late payments are $5.00 per day.**</u>

Rate increases will take effect _____

In the event I am not able to work, when possible, _____ will provide substitute care.

Do NOT bring children with diarrhea, vomiting, fever, or rash.

Parents are responsible for formula, diapers, wipes, pull-ups, a change of clothes, and all other necessary supplies.

Parents are encouraged to visit or call any time.

Parents are welcome in any area of my home any time that childcare is being provided.

No child will be discriminated against for any reason!

<u>Children will be exposed to Christian based materials.</u>

<u>Children will be exposed to animals.</u>

I AM A MANDATED REPORTER OF SUSPECTED CHILD ABUSE AND SEX TRAFFICKING BEHAVIOR.

The first ten days of care are probationary for provider, parent, and child.

_____   _____
Provider Signature   Date   Parent Signature   Date

Policies should be your procedures that parents need to know about. Discipline, health and safety and emergency plans are super important to explain in your policies. They should explain what your expectations are and what you provide. I have my parents sign a sheet that they read and understand them and keep it in my files.

My policies include our emergency procedures for multiple scenarios because in Oklahoma we are required by DHS to have policies on them. They also include medication policies, my training, rules for the kids, discipline, and anything parents need to know.

There is an editable template of my policies you can change to make your own in the document pack.

Vacation planning and days off

You will have to decide if you are going to have paid holidays off or paid vacation days. I like to set my vacation days in January for the whole year. This gives families plenty of time to plan and make arrangements. I send out reminders at the beginning of the month if I have any days off that month so if anyone forgets they have time to make new plans.

I try to stick to just these days off, but we are human and some things come up. We get sick, our family needs us, or other things that can't be helped. Once every few years I have to take off unexpectedly.

You'll also need to make a plan for a substitute. In Oklahoma we are required to have one. Mine is my husband but I hardly ever use him. If I need to renew my driver's license or something that just takes a few minutes, I let my families know I'm going to run the errand and then I try to do it during nap. If they don't want my husband to watch their kids, they can keep them at home that day. I only do it about once every two years or so when it can't be helped.

If you are open in communicating with your families, you are going to have a good relationship with most people and your business will grow and be successful.

Check the document pack for an editable copy of the business policies.

Business Policies

Owner/Operator:

EMERGENCY PHONE NUMBERS

Emergency Medical Care

Police/Fire/Ambulance   911

Other Important Numbers

DHS Licensing

Child Abuse Hotline

County Emergency Management

Information   411

Poison Control   1-800-222-1222

Police/Fire Non-Emergency

Road Conditions

Department of Mental Health and Substance Abuse

Utilities

    Electric

    Water

    Gas

Emergency Contact

    1 in town and one out of town

Quick Reference

The list below provides direction in particular situations. Refer to the section(s) indicated for specific procedures.

IMMEDIATE EVACUATION

- Smoke
- Fire (or explosion)
- Gas Leak
- Bomb Threat

EVACUATION AND RELOCATION

- Hazardous Spill
- Chemical/Industrial Accident
- Flood
- Wildfire

SHELTER IN PLACE

- Tornado
- Dangerous High Winds
- Earthquake
- Blizzard
- Ice Storm
- Terrorist Attack
- Bomb/War
- Biological Attack
- Armed Intruder/Attacker
- Hostage Situation
- Radiological Emergency

The emergency evacuation pack is located in the storage room closet.

Children with special needs will be attended to include insuring any medications that are on site for a child will be taken with the child in the event of the emergency relocation of the facility staff and children.

Utility disruptions require children be picked up after 2 hours without power or when temperatures inside facility reach over 85 or under 60 degrees.

EVACUATION AND RELOCATION

Evacuation: Smoke, Fire, Gas Leak or Bomb Threat

There are several hazardous situations that could call for an evacuation. The most common would be a fire in or near the facility, rising flood waters, or an evacuation order issued by the local police, fire, or other governmental authority. A verbal order to evacuate for any other reason will be given by me. Children will be accounted for visually and with a head count upon departure from the home and upon arrival to the_____. This allows for a safe distance from the threat and room for emergency responders. Secondary location will be _____.

I will grab the emergency pack, and lead children. Once we are safe, I will call emergency services. If children cannot be safely evacuated, emergency personnel will be immediately notified of who is in the building and where. Once children are safe and accounted for, I will notify parents immediately and we will remain clear of the building.

Relocation: Hazardous Spills, Chemical/Industrial Accidents, Flood, Wildfire

If the entire area has to be evacuated due to a hazard announced by Emergency Personnel (law enforcement, fire department, emergency services personnel, national guard), staff and children will be moved to _____. I will insure a notice of the relocation is posted on the entry to the facility which includes contact information. I will secure children in vehicle as safely as possible and grab emergency pack. On arrival at _____, I will notify parents or guardians to come get their children. Secondary location will _____.

Evacuation or relocation will always be done by me unless I am incapacitated. _____ will be trained in the procedures as well.

In any evacuation or relocation, all children will be accounted for at the start, and again, at the completion. During any evacuation, a quick assessment of the situation will be made. Minor injuries to staff or children will be cared for as soon as time permits.

Children will not be released except to an identified authorized pick up person.

Transportation in an emergency will be provided by myself in my _____ and _____ in their _____.

EVACUATION AND RELOCATION CHECKLIST

☐ Grab emergency bag

☐ Evacuate children and other individuals in the home

☐ Attach notice to entrance area

☐ Secure children in a safe place

☐ Call 911 from outside the home

☐ Take attendance, search for anyone missing

☐ Have the following items ready for emergency responders

- Number of children
- Knowledge of anyone remaining inside
- Floor plan

☐ Notify parents for pick up

☐ Calm the children and address their needs

☐ Notify licensing

☐ Write incident report after incident is complete

SHELTER IN PLACE OR LOCKDOWN

Tornado, Dangerous High Winds, Earthquake, Blizzard, Ice Storm, Terrorist Attack, Bomb/War, Biological Attack, Radiological Emergency, Armed Intruder/Attacker, Hostage Situation

Weather Emergencies:

    Tornado or Dangerous High Winds:

    ☐ Get inside if outside

    ☐ Account for all children

    ☐ Lock all doors and windows and close blinds/curtains

    ☐ Shelter children in _____

    ☐ Stay away from windows

    ☐ Calm children and address needs

    ☐ Contact parents when possible

    Earthquakes:

    ☐ If outside, get away from buildings and structures

    ☐ If inside, shelter children under kitchen table.

    ☐ Account for all children

    ☐ Calm children and address needs

    ☐ Contact parents when possible

    Blizzard/Ice Storms:

    ☐ Watch weather reports closely

    ☐ Calm children and address needs

Terrorist Attack, Bomb/War, Biological Attack, Radiological Emergency, Armed Intruder/Attacker, Hostage Situation:

☐ Get inside if outside

☐ Account for all children

☐ Lock all doors and windows and close blinds/curtains

☐ Shelter children in _____

☐ Stay away from windows

☐ Calm children and address needs

☐ Call 911 for help

☐ Contact parents when possible

☐ Notify licensing after event

☐ Write incident report after incident is complete

ASSAULT ON CHILD OR STAFF

☐ Call 911

☐ Administer CPR/First Aid as necessary

☐ Follow lockdown procedures

☐ Notify parents

☐ Notify licensing

☐ Write incident report after incident is complete

MISSING CHILD

☐ In the event I identify a child as missing, I will immediately call 911.

☐ Search for child again

☐ Call the child's parent or guardian. If the parent or guardian is not reached the emergency contact persons on the child's enrollment form will be called. Attempts will be made to contact the child's parent or guardian; or emergency contact, until one of them has been contacted.

☐ Insure all other children, who are supposed to be there, are verified to be in the facility.

☐ I will insure each child in their care is in the indoor care area with them pending further direction.

☐ Cooperate with law enforcement in the search for the missing child. Provide information and photo of child to law enforcement.

☐ Notify licensing.

POISONING

☐ Call poison control 1-800-222-1222

☐ Follow instructions given

☐ Call 911 if necessary

☐ Notify parents when possible

☐ Notify licensing

☐ Write incident report after incident is complete

EXPULSION POLICY

_____ reserves the right to expel students at any time for any reason. Some of these reasons may include, but <u>are not</u> limited to:

Safety of children in care or provider

Lack of compliance with contract and policies such as negligent payment history, not abiding by business hours, etc.

Disrespect for provider or care provided.

Any other reason provider feels expulsion is necessary.

Name of Child:

I have read and understand these policies.

Name:

_____

Signature

My enrollment policy is pretty unique. I do a home visit before I enroll a child. When a potential parent contacts me, I do an initial visit with them over the phone. If we both think things might work well between us, I schedule a time for them to come visit.

I schedule it when the kids are here. I give them a tour, talk to them and the child a bit, answer any questions they have and ask questions about the child. I want them to get a good picture of what I have to offer. I like to watch the child interact with the other kids a little bit too.

Then if they are still interested and I am, I give them a packet of paperwork and schedule a second interview at their house. This gives the child a chance to see me in their home and know that I'm a safe person. It helps with separation anxiety. I like to see their favorite toy and meet their pets. I also want to meet everyone in the family including dad and siblings. I play with the child for a bit at their house. This helps us bond.

If people are not interested in letting me come over, I'm not interested in doing business with them. This weeds out a lot of potential problems. Later, when the child starts, if they are upset when their parents leave, I will ask them about their doggy or their favorite stuffed animal and they remember the time we spent together. It helps them feel safe.

Spending more time on the interview helps the parents feel safe too. It gives us time to get to know each other.

The interview with daycare families should be personal, friendly and relaxed to give them an opportunity to ask any questions they may have or share information with you that you need. You should present yourself as a professional and let parents know of your training and education. They won't know all the work you've put into being awesome if you don't tell them.

The interview is the time you need to go over the contract with parents (and policies too) to make sure they understand them. Communicate the rules to families and let them know which ones are most important to you. What is your deal breaker?

There are some important things that need to be in the interview packet:

Contract (2 copies, one for them to keep and one for you to keep)

Policies and form that says they read and understand them

Food paperwork

DHS child information form (if you don't have these requirements where you live, make a form that has names, addresses, contact info, work information and who is allowed to pick up the child and their contact info. It should also have any health problems or allergies)

Medication permission form

Permission to transport form (or not to)

Other required forms for licensure where you live

Media release if you will be sharing photos on social media

Copy of your cycle menu

Copy of your goals for the year

Copy of your days off

Business card or something with your contact info on it

Chapter 11-Routines for daycare success

You'll need a basic schedule to go by to keep your days on track. For us, DHS and the food program set the basic structure. We have to have our meals within 15 minutes of the planned time and nap is necessary for growing kids.

You have opening time and closing time, meals and nap to outline the day. You need a meal every three hours unless the kids are asleep.

Here's a sample:

7:00	Open
7:00-8:30	Child Directed Play (kids arrive at different times)
8:30-9:00	Breakfast
9:00-9:15	Clean up breakfast, potty, wash up

9:15-10:15 In hot summer months we go straight outside at this time. We work in the garden and play. Sometimes we have activities outside as well. In the cold winter months, we do activities inside at this time and have free play until about 10:00 so it warms up a bit outside first.

10:15-10:30	Potty, wash up
10:30-11:00	Activities (or outside time)
11:00-11:30	Movie time while Ms. Christina makes lunch
11:30-12:00	Lunch
12:00-12:15	Clean up lunch, potty, wash up
12:15-12:45	Stories, songs and fingerplays
12:45-3:00	Nap or rest for those who don't fall asleep
3:00-3:15	Snack
3:15-3:30	Clean up snack, potty, wash up
3:30-5:00	Child directed play (everyone goes home at different times)

There is an editable schedule in the document pack.

Child directed play can be me reading to them if they ask (which they do a lot), puzzles, blocks, playing with the special toy or just the stuff that's out all the time like trucks, cars, dishes, kitchen, tools, dress up, dolls, etc. If they ask for an activity, I will usually get it for them.

Our special toy is something they pick on Mondays that we use throughout the week during free time. I have a train set, a set of boats and balls, Lincoln logs, potato heads, garages and cars, Legos, benders, farms, doll house, emergency centers (hospital, fire station and police station) and several other choices.

We have a star every day. The child who is the star gets to bless the food at meals, choose the movie they watch while I cook lunch, sit in a special chair, eat off a mickey mouse plate, and choose the special toy. If we get a package, they get to get it from the delivery people and carry it to my bed.

They are the star and get to do all the special privileges for that day. This way everyone gets a turn to be special. I have a chart on the fridge and I move a magnet every day to keep track.

Activities include school on Mondays, science on Tuesdays, music and free art on Wednesdays, and different things on Thursday. Fridays are fun Fridays and we have more free play time.

For school we practice spelling our names, trace lines on paper, practice saying our phone numbers, play with ABC puzzles or books and talk about letters, count stuff and things like that.

For science we do all kinds of different things. Maybe mix colors of paint or playdough, do gardening stuff, plant seeds, learn about bugs, play with magnets, cook, go on a nature walk and observe with magnifying glasses or any number of things.

Music is hopping music of the kid's choosing and musical instruments. There is lots of dancing and fun times. Then we have paper and different art mediums. Kids can choose whatever they want to create with what I give them. It might be crayons, colored pencils, markers, rainbow crayons, glue and collage materials or any number of things. They create whatever they want.

On Thursdays we may do something like make a book, every once in a while, we make a craft, we might have another free art project like painting or scratch cards, could be any number of things.

You can focus on whatever works for you and your group. This I just an idea of what you could do. Just remember, a little planning ahead helps a lot in sticking to what you wanted to accomplish.

I plan the whole school year at once. I spend about a month working on it and getting everything ready. If I don't plan ahead, I won't stick to what I wanted to do with the kids. I plan the summer all at once as well. We do this preschool schedule from around the first of September and keep it up until around the end of May.

In May and August, we have a few weeks of all free time before getting back to structured plans. This is the time I use to really get the planning done. In August and September, we have kids leaving for school and new kids coming in, so there is plenty of chaos to be had.

Making sure you have scheduled potty times helps with potty training as well.

The structure you use for your day helps keep you sane. We don't always to every single thing we plan, but for the most part, we keep learning and moving forward.

In the summer I do more free time and more special events. We usually have a party of some sort every few weeks. Might be a [dinosaur party](), super hero week, color week, pirate party, week long study of bees, pond study, whatever I come up with. There are tons of ideas for themes and special parties on the blog if you want to get some ideas.

One thing I always make sure of is not to spend a ton of money. Most of our party favors and props are homemade. We make dinoculars to hunt dinos out of cut paper towel and wrapping paper tubes. I don't like wasting resources or money, so I try to keep things simple. Spending is a minimum. I don't make much so I have to protect my family's budget.

The kids can draw pictures to decorate the walls. You can make paper chains with them for more party décor. We did a volcano for our dinosaur party last year and I just dug a hole in the back yard and piled up dirt around it instead of using resources that would have to be thrown away. The kids got to pour the vinegar into the volcano and all I had to do to clean it up was throw the dirt from the sides back into the hole. It was nearly free.

Being creative with what little resources you have is a great way to get more out of it. What are you good at? Make a party out of that. I happen to be awesome at making paper airplanes. My dad was an engineer and he built airplanes for Boeing. That was one thing we had a nice time doing together. And he taught me some mad skills.

I have always fashioned tons of off the chain airplanes for my kids in kid's church, my daughter and my daycare kids. This summer we are going to have an airplane week with a paper airplane party at the end. I am going to make up a bunch and tape them to the walls and the kids can take them home for party favors. We are also going to color papers and fold them into airplanes at the party.

The kids will LOVE a paper airplane party and it will only cost me a package of paper. Plus, I'm going to have fun making a bunch of different designs for the kids AND teaching them about aerodynamics and wind lift and stuff. I'm stoked.

Do what works for you in your schedule. If your bag is music, you can have music with instruments, dance offs, make instruments, teach the kids to yodel, learn about different genres of music or anything you want to do. We love to have dance parties to chase the grumpies away.

Keep the focus interesting to you and the children.

Get a refrigerator box and let the kids decorate it and make a play house. Make a boat. Make a castle. Make a race car. Whatever you and your kids come up with will work great. You don't need to be just like another provider. You don't need to follow anyone else's goals or plans. Make your daycare into what you enjoy.

Cleaning schedule

There is tons of cleaning in daycare. You'll need to keep up with all the things the kids dirty up and it's not easy.

Sheets and bedding materials need to be cleaned weekly.

Toys need to be sanitized weekly.

Toys that are mouthed or used a lot need to be cleaned daily.

Dress up clothes and stuffed animals need to be laundered every few weeks.

The kitchen and dining areas need to be cleaned and sanitized multiple times a day.

Windows that kids lick (yes lick) at least weekly.

The floors need to be cleaned daily. We sweep, vacuum and steam the floors every night.

The changing table needs to be sanitized after each use. (especially between kids)

The bathroom needs to be wiped down and sanitized daily (you'll be surprised how messy it can get) and scrubbed weekly or twice a week.

Floors should be scanned and picked up several times a day to keep choking hazards away from kids.

I am allergic to bleach so I sanitize with vinegar. The bleach solution is 1 quart of water to 1 ½ teaspoons of bleach. Bleach loses it's bleachiness in water after 24 hours so it has to be mixed every day. This is an inexpensive solution except you'll have to replace your sprayers regularly because the bleach eats the insides of them out.

Spray your sanitizer on your surfaces and let stand for one minute. Then wipe off.

Then there's your regular cleaning on top of that. It can be overwhelming, but you'll get into a routine and it will become habit. Before parents come in the morning and at pick up time, make sure your porch and entry way in the house is free of obstacles and looking tidy.

This will help you keep business. I don't know how many parents have complained to me about people's houses looking junky or dirty, and it's just the habit of plopping things by the front door. The image people first see when they walk up is important.

Paperwork

In and out sheets need to be done daily

Food paperwork needs to be done daily

Enrollment forms need to be done before kids begin care.

Yearly contracts, food enrollment forms and other forms need to be done at the same time every year. We have updated insurance forms and compliance file forms that have to be renewed every year. We do ours Sept 1. Rate increases take place Sept 1. Everything starts over in September, so I can always remember to do it all at once when new kids are enrolling and kids are leaving for preschool.

Emergency drills need to be done and recorded monthly and some yearly. Smoke detectors need to be tested monthly and recorded as well.

Daily reports for kids, especially infants need to be done daily. These tell how the child's day was, and especially for infants when they ate, how much and if they pooped. You can record each diaper but knowing how often a child poops is important to keep track of their health and when two people are providing care at different times (parents and providers) that can be missed if it's not recorded.

Tax receipts and utilities should be logged monthly or bi weekly so you don't have time to forget what you bought or what it was for.

Medication forms and logs should be filled out when medicine is brought and every time medication is given.

Records to keep track of your training should be filled out when training is received and reviewed periodically to make sure you are getting enough training. Everyone should learn as much as they can, but in Oklahoma, the minimum requirements for training is 12 hours a year or 20 hours a year for stars participants. Those logs are reviewed at licensing visits.

If you have any certificates or degrees you need to keep track of the records of those and what you need to renew and how much training is required.

Feel free to use the editable schedules in the document pack.

Daycare Cleaning Schedule

Multiple x daily	Kitchen cleaned and sanitized
	Changing table sanitized
	Scan and pick up floors
Daily	Toys that kids put in their mouths
	Sweep, vacuum and mop or steam floors
Weekly	Sheets and bedding
	Sanitize all toys
	Windows
	Bathrooms
Twice monthly	Dress up clothes and stuffed animals

Daycare Paperwork Schedule

Daily	In and out sheets
	Food paperwork
	Daily reports for kids
As occurs	Medication permission and logs
	Enrollment forms before child begins care
	Training records
Monthly	Log all tax receipts and utility bills
	Emergency drills
	Immunization records reviewed
Yearly	Contracts, policies and other enrollment forms should be updated

Chapter 12: Advertising

The next step after getting your home and paperwork in order and getting inspected and licensed is to <u>advertise.</u> Before you have a reputation for your business, you'll have to come up with some ways you can get customers. You can use craigslist, Facebook, newspaper ads, flyers you can hang at pediatricians and other places people take kids, CARE.COM, and many other places.

There is a great article on the blog that will give you some creative ideas to get your name out there.

Remember that word of mouth is the best way to get business, so tell your friends, talk about it at church, go by the nursery and let the workers know, ask your kid's teachers if anyone is looking, talk to the secretary in the office, and have your friends talk about it to their friends at work.

You'll get your name out there in no time. Put it on your Facebook page. Tell people what you plan to offer and what's special about you and your business.

Always remember that everything you do with your clients and how to treat each person will be talked about in the future. Don't forget to be professional and businesslike in your every day interactions with everyone.

Once you get <u>licensed</u> and set to open and you advertise, now you are ready to open your doors

Chapter 13: Open your business

Now you have kids enrolled, a start date, you're certified, you have toys and supplies at the ready, a menu prepared and the food bought, paperwork filled out and your schedule set. You're ready to provide childcare.

It's going to be exhausting. You'll have to get into a rhythm to be able to keep up with everything. But you'll know within 2-3 weeks if this gig is for you. If you're exhausted, that's to be expected. If you're exhausted and you don't have any fun. Maybe it's not right for you.

Be easy with your schedule at first. Make sure you hit your meals and nap but don't worry if you don't get anything else done. Just the potty and diaper situation are enough to overwhelm a newbie. You'll get there.

Once you get in the routine of the basics, then you can start adding a few activities in every week. The kids will be getting used to the toys you have and they'll be ready for more to entertain them too. They'll have had a chance to get to know you and each other.

Avoiding burnout

Burnout in childcare is super high. The reason is because the hours are long, the pay is low, the work is hard and people don't appreciate it much. If you are going to do child care, make sure you are ready for all of that. Have a plan in place to take care of yourself and make sure you stay well physically and mentally.

Make sure you schedule breaks for yourself. Use relaxation techniques. Treat yourself and be kind to yourself. Stay encouraged. If you can't, quit. It's better to do something else than to do this job poorly. It requires your best.

Make sure you drink enough water and stay hydrated. Avoid living off caffeine or other stimulants to keep you going. Eat nutritious food that gives you energy. Get regular exercise and stay active in other ways that rejuvenate you after long hard hours.

There's a lot more on the blog about stress, burnout and staying motivated. Check it out.

Another great way to make sure you stay motivated is by joining groups. Find a local childcare organization where you can network with other providers. No one else understands the stress this job can put on you, not even your spouse. You NEED provider friends.

Another way to connect is on Facebook groups like Daycare Providers Rock or Everything Home Daycare. Join them and share ideas with the people there. It may make the difference between loving and hating the job.

Chapter 14: Record keeping

Like you saw in the schedule and routine chapter, there is a lot of paperwork that needs to be kept.

You need records for the kids you are keeping. Their food allergies, health conditions, parent info, who is allowed to pick them up, etc.

If you're on a food program, you'll need a set of food paperwork for them.

Your menu and maybe shopping lists if you want to make things easier day to day.

Keeping records will save you money. You won't lose tax deductions or other benefits from having great records. You should review all your records periodically, monthly is a good idea. Save all your daycare records for 3 years in case you need to refer back to them.

You need to keep your tax receipts and information for 7 years. I have heard all kinds of advice on this, some people say 3, some say 10. To be safe, you can keep them for 10 and you'll never have to worry.

Most of the record keeping involved in daycare has to do with taxes.

Taxes

What is deductible? Ordinary and necessary for business is the definition of deductible. Think about the obvious like scissors and crayons for the kids, but also think about the not so obvious like pictures for the wall. If you didn't have your house decorated nicely, would you have business? No. So it's a necessary expense. Now, you won't be able to claim 100% of that picture like you would crayons, but you can claim your time space percentage of it or actual business use. We'll get into what that means later.

You must keep adequate records to support your deductions. Save receipts for all expenses associated with your house. Keep records of all meals and snacks served even if you didn't claim them on the food program.

Track all the hours you work in your home.

You will owe taxes on all income you receive in your business. That includes money your parents give you directly, but it also includes subsidy money, grants, food program reimbursements and even gifts you receive.

Home expenses include: Rent, mortgage interest, property taxes, utilities, house insurance, home repairs, fencing, landscaping, etc.

Food-what you get reimbursed for and what you don't. If you have a party for your daycare families on Saturday, the food expense from that counts as well.

Supplies include: Toys, outdoor play equipment, art supplies, books, CD's, diapers, field trip expenses, Christmas gifts and birthday gifts for the kids, sleep mats, bedding, cribs, swings, balls, bottles, dishes, bibs, anything at all that you purchase to use with the kids. If you have kids of your own at home, you'll only be able to claim part of the items they use along with the other kids.

Household items: Toilet paper, paper towels, cleaning supplies, light bulbs, tools kitchen supplies, yard supplies, laundry detergent, dish soap, mops, brooms, garden hoses, etc. Furniture and appliances are partially deductible such as a rocker, microwave, refrigerator, freezer, washer, dryer, tables, rugs, beds, chairs, tv, etc.

There are many other expenses you can deduct that don't fit into these main categories such as: Advertising, liability insurance, dues, training, computer and printer, car expenses and so many more. I recommend getting Tom Copeland's book on Family Childcare Record Keeping. It's a must have resource.

Vehicle expenses: Keep track of all mileage you drive in your car for business purposes. You can track the mileage to the grocery store for instance, and then use your grocery receipts at the end of the year to multiply it by how many times you went there. If you buy your family's food with the daycare food, you can deduct half of those trips. If you take the kids to the park, you can record that mileage and multiply it by the number of times you went there.

Keep track of all the meals served to kids, who was in attendance and what you served. If you're on the food program, you'll already have this paperwork available. If not, you'll need to create documents to record all of it for tax purposes.

Keeping records regularly helps you get the most deductions because you don't have time to forget everything you've done. You can also use your planning calendar to remember a lot of the activities you did.

You will need to pay in for your taxes quarterly. You'll have to do an estimated tax form 1040ES in April, June, September and January.

If you hire someone to work in your daycare, you'll have to withhold payroll taxes on them. Tom Copeland's books can help you with this process as well.

I have a drawer I throw all my receipts in until I have time to record them. It helps to have a central location for them. You'll be so glad you did.

You'll also need to save all cancelled checks, credit card statements, calendars, food program forms and bank statements.

Keep good records for the best tax outcome possible. At least monthly, log your home utilities, your receipts you collected, and your income received. It's not complicated to record it. Just make a spread sheet on the computer or a piece of paper. Make columns for the expense categories listed above. Take each receipt and log it into what category it goes in. Make sure to make two columns for supplies. One for 100% business and one for a percentage business.

One hundred percent business will be the things that are only for daycare. Percentage for the shared expenses with your family. Remember, if your own kids use it, it's shared. The percentage you get to deduct depends on several things. You'll need to get Tom Copeland's Family Childcare Tax Workbook for help figuring percentages or have your tax preparer show you.

At the end of the year, if you have this done, it makes tax time so much easier. Trust me, I've tried it both ways.

Filling out the forms for daycare taxes is fairly complicated. You can do it yourself if you use Tom Copeland's tax workbook. You can also hire a professional. I would recommend one of these two things. It's a pretty massive undertaking and you need some type of guidance. If you do hire a professional, realize that most tax preparers are not familiar with tax laws concerning daycare homes, so you may want to get the workbook for your tax preparer anyway.

When hiring a tax preparer, ask questions about how much they know about home daycare rules and make sure you find someone who can do an adequate job for you. Otherwise you may end up paying far more than necessary.

Conclusion

Daycare is a tough job, but if it's meant for you, you'll love it like nothing else. I cannot imagine doing anything else with my life. I've learned so much over the past 23 years, and I never stop learning. There are always things I can do better. There's always something I can change.

I love kids and I love that we get to make memories together in this gig. I love how they talk to me and tell me things. I love how they love me. I love their precious little hearts and the funny things they say.

I encourage you, if your heart is drawn towards being your own boss and making a difference in the world, to try out daycare if you think it's right for you. You may fall in love with it like I have. If you do and you put your whole heart into it, you'll be a legacy in your community and you'll set up the future with something good.

I have teenagers and grown people who talk about my influence and how much they love me. I have high school teachers tell me they can tell when kids came from my house to school. I have preschool and kindergarten teachers that say the same. I KNOW I'm making a difference. I know I'm preparing kids for the future. I know I'm doing what I'm meant to do.

If you have any questions or comments, feel free to contact me by email at christina@littlesproutslearning.co or on Facebook at Raising Happy Healthy Kids. I'd love to hear from you. Please leave a review where you purchased this guide and let people know what you think. Thank you!

Happy caregiving! You're going to rock it!

Free Printable Templates available in the document pack:

Daycare Checklist

Daycare Income Calculator

Daycare Menu Sample and Template

Daycare Cleaning and Paperwork Schedules

Daycare Daily Report

Daycare Daily Schedule

Business Policies

Contract for Childcare Services

Medication Permission Form

Multimedia Permission Form

Multimedia Permission Form

The password to access the document pack is docupack. I hope it's a super helpful tool for you!

Thank you for reading. We encourage you to share your thoughts and reactions.

RESOURCES

Little Sprouts Learning Blog full of information on gardening with kids, cooking with kids, feeding kids healthy food, parenting and provider tips.

https://littlesproutslearning.co/

Tom Copeland's blog with links to all his record keeping and tax workbooks.

http://tomcopelandblog.com/

Dr. Becky Bailey's Website with links to all her Conscious Discipline Books.

https://consciousdiscipline.com/about/becky-bailey/

Reggio Emilia teaching method.

https://www.reggioalliance.org/

Food Program information.

https://www.fns.usda.gov/cacfp/family-day-care-homes

Regulations by state.

https://childcareta.acf.hhs.gov/licensing

Author Bio

Christina Kamp has been a family child care provider with a successful business for over 23 years. She has been helping other providers get started and find success in their businesses too. She LOVES kids and the field of child care and wants to see more providers loving what they do.

Christina is married and has a daughter that is 27 years old. She has kept over 80 children during her child care career which has always been an in-home daycare.

Christina has earned her Child Development Associate Credential, has been nationally accredited through National Association for Family Child Care for 12 years, and has worked hard at being the best provider she can be. She has grown a very successful business that is always as full as she wants it to be with a long waiting list.

Christina feels that child care is her calling and she takes it very seriously. It's the most important job in the world.

Made in United States
Orlando, FL
20 June 2024